THE 7 P'S OF PUBLISHING SUCCESS

Mark Leslie Lefebvre

Stark Publishing Solutions

Copyright © 2018 by Mark Leslie Lefebvre

Author photo © 2018 Lauren Lang, Jacobin Photography
"Rocket education" cover image © 2018 Dharshani Gk Arts via Dreamstime.com

All rights reserved. No part of this publication may be reproduced, distributed or transmitted in any form or by any means, without prior written permission.

Stark Publishing Solutions

An Imprint of Stark Publishing
Waterloo, Ontario
www.starkpublishing.ca

Publisher's Note: This work is derived from the author's experience in bookselling, writing and publishing and is meant to inform and inspire writers with tools and strategies for success in their own writing path. The author and publisher believe that there is no single magic solution for everyone and that advice, wisdom and insights should be carefully curated and adapted to suit each individual's needs, goals and desires.

The 7 P's of Publishing Success / Mark Leslie Lefebvre
September 2018

Print ISBN: 978-1-7751478-1-7
eBook ISBN: 978-1-7751478-2-4
Audio ISBN: 978-1-7751478-3-1

Praise for Mark Leslie Lefebvre

Mark was a critical hire at a critical time for Kobo. We knew independent publishing was a growing phenomenon in eBooks but needed the right person to create that all-important bridge with the author community. Mark performed that role perfectly, winning authors over to *Kobo Writing Life* with his combination of energy, lived experience as an author, genuine enthusiasm for how technology could extend a writer's reach. A truly valuable person.
    —Michael Tamblyn, *CEO at Rakuten Kobo, Inc.*

Mark was a regular guest speaker for our students in the Creative Writing Program, at SFU Continuing Studies. His talks balanced providing encouraging information with the business realities of publishing. Our writers went away feeling excited about the publishing opportunities available to them, but also understood that though it is simple to publish through KWL or Amazon, success requires hard work. I personally enjoyed each one of Mark's presentations and would learn something new each time.
    —Andrew Chesham, *Simon Fraser University*

His broad knowledge of publishing provided me with valuable contacts, referencematerials and a couple of great ideas to move my writing and publishing projects forward. I highly recommend any way you can find time to spend with him - great value at half the price you'd expect!
    — Mark Jones, *Author*

Mark is a pro. His decades of experience and continuing relevance (staying on the leading edge of publishing is no small feat in this climate) is a major asset to anyone looking to improve their position in the market...and not drive themselves insane in the process. That is gold. He is genuine, innovative, smart and seriously easy to work with. Highly recommend booking his 20-minute free consult, it can change everything.
    — Sarah Kades Author

Other Books in this Series

Killing It on Kobo

Leverage Insights to Optimize Publishing and Marketing Strategies, Grow Global Sales and Increase Revenue on Kobo
October 2018

Indie Publishing Insider Secrets

Insights, Wisdom and Stark Perspectives on Writing, Publishing and Bookselling Success From a 25 Year Book Industry Professional
Coming Early 2019

*This one goes out to the P's I left behind
(Yes, that's meant to be an #earworm)*

Table of Contents

INTRODUCTION: From 3 P's to 7 9

PRACTICE 13

PROFESSIONALISM 17

PATIENCE 29

PROGRESSION 35

PERSISTENCE 41

PARTNERSHIP 47

PATRONAGE 51

PROMOTION 59

CONCLUSION 61

RESOURCES 63

ABOUT THE AUTHOR 65

INTRODUCTION: From 3 P's to 7

WHEN I FIRST started traveling around the world and speaking to authors about writing and publishing success for Kobo Writing Life, I came up with what I called the "3 P's of Self-Publishing Success." They were *Patience*, *Practice* and *Persistence*. After sharing and then briefly explaining what each of them meant, I would remind the audience that those elements were not all that different than what it took to be successful in traditional publishing.

I enjoyed drawing comparisons between those two paths, which, in 2011, when I really started to make the rounds in the writing and publishing community speaking circuit, were quite diverse.

Now, of course, they aren't necessarily diverse and separate paths; they are more intertwined and complex, as authors understand the benefits of taking a hybrid approach to their writing and publishing journey.

Just a few months after I left Kobo at the end of 2017, I agreed to do a talk for them at a writing seminar that focused on the business of writing. As I reviewed the slides that were sent to me for the presentation I was giving on behalf of Kobo Writing Life, I spotted a version of my 3 Ps' in the deck.

It was like looking at an ex lover, an old flame. I felt a sense of nostalgia for it; I was reminded of the good times we had together, of the shared memories of the two of us working together helping to enlighten writers' lives.

But, in that same manner, I saw how I had grown since first creating it; or, to follow the "old flame" analogy, how we had both grown in different directions, still appreciating what brought us together, but also appreciating how our paths diverted.

I was reminded of how I had drafted those original 3 P's up in about five minutes, likely either the night before or perhaps even an hour before I took the stage sometime in late 2011 or early 2012 and then had continued to use those same P's in various other talks over the years. I had taken that hastily drafted concept for granted over the years, but I hadn't really taken a longer, more reflective look at it.

It's funny how, when you look at something from the outside, you begin to see it in a new light. This, of course, is one of the reasons why an editor brings such value to a writer. It's not just their skills related to language, grammar and story; it's the fresh and outside perspective they bring.

So, I sat back, and I admired this concept, this structure.

I am, after all, a fan of alliteration. (Sorry, I really should have said that *I admire, adore and advise alliteration, and am an ally to its application.* There, that feels more *applicable*)

So, ever since I delivered this concept, this old flame, for the KWL team, I've been reflecting on it and finding a new perspective on it that is different than when I first created it. Elements that I suppose I missed when first drafting it together. Yes, those three elements of *Patience, Practice* and *Persistence* are still definitely true. And I had ordered them in a way that sounded better rolling off my tongue. It was something I could easily conjure up when a writer would ask me for short and quick tidbits of advice; the three words could easily be rhymed off, always in that order.

But I began to realize that those were merely almost half of the overall picture of success.

Yes, the three elements were necessary ingredients, likely the core or underlying foundation for a writer to build to success. But there was more.

After reflecting on my career representing self-publishing, digital publishing and bookselling and all the information I had read, listened to, and participated in sharing, I determined that something was missing.

I needed more P's.

And I needed to re-order them.

And so, here are all 7 of them, in what I feel is a more natural order:

Practice

Professionalism

Patience

Progression

Persistence

Partnership

Patronage

There's even a bonus P thrown in there for good measure: *Promotion*.

Within each element I will share stories from both my own experience as well as examples from writers I know and whose own journeys I have followed over the years to help illustrate each P.

I hope you get as much benefit out of them as I received from the process of reflecting upon and outlining the value of each.

But that's enough introductory chatter. Let's get into the very first P.

PRACTICE

THE FIRST ELEMENT of publishing success falls in line with what might be the most common advice that successful authors from both traditional publishing and self-publishing share when asked by beginning writers.

"First, write a good book."

It's a simple thing to say, a basic principle to understand, but it is often overlooked.

The more you write, the better you become at writing.

Therefore, writing a good book means practicing and working at becoming better at your craft by actually planting your butt in a chair and getting those fingers to dance across your keyboard.

Malcolm Gladwell brought the concept of 10,000 Hours to popular culture several years ago. He argued that studies revealed how it would take approximately ten thousand hours of actually performing or practicing a skill in order to become a master of it. There are all kinds of counter arguments to Gladwell's assumptions, including the task itself, the basic, initial skill, and whether or not a person is willing to learn, or re-learn something they thought that they knew. I address that a bit further in the element of Progression but for now, let's go back to the simple premise.

The more you write, the better you become at it.

As you continue to write, as you continue to read, all of those efforts and moments and time spent working at both consuming and creating narratives are cumulative. Today when you sit down to write, you are that much more experienced than you were when you sat down to do it yesterday. The difference, of course, from day to day, is virtually imperceptible. But the difference, over months and years, might be a bit easier to see. Because, if you have practiced, and continued to exercise those writing muscles, you are a better writer today than you were when you first started.

If, like me, you still have early writing efforts kicking around in a drawer or file folders, go and take a look at them and compare them with the things you are writing today. Perhaps these are your very first attempts at writing a story, or maybe they are the essays or stories you wrote as part of elementary school assignments. Take a look at how your writing has grown, changed and developed as you have matured as a writer; as you have practiced and gotten better as a writer.

The more you write, the more you exercise those writing muscles, or, in other words, the more you practice applying all of those elements of grammar and style, character and setting, descriptions, dialogue, and plot that you uniquely combine to create our distinct writer voice. And the more you tone those muscles, the more natural all of those elements of writing are employed each time that you sit down to write.

The key is to make it a habit.

You need to write every day. I was going to end that last sentence with "if possible" merely to acknowledge that there will be some days where you get no writing done. But I didn't add "if possible" to it because that leaves an easy "out" that I don't want to just leave sitting there that I know a writer will cling to as part of the "resistance" to getting the writing done that can be so common. Writing needs to be a regular habit for you. It needs to be something that you do regularly, like brushing your teeth or showering (and, oh yes, these are part of another element of writing success that I'll get to in the next chapter). It is an essential part of you and who you are. Writing needs to be something that you can't not do. It needs to be harder for you not to write than it is to write.

One of my favourite quotes about writing comes from Hugh Prather and I have had it posted near my writing space for almost thirty years.

"If the desire to write is not accompanied by actual writing, then the desire is not to write."

Write. Write some more. And after that, write even more.

One of the other things that you will find if you make a habit of writing every day, is that you'll have more work, more completed projects, and more publishable material.

Because that's the secondary and positive side-effect of so much writing; of so much practice.

More stories. More books.

Based on my decades long bookselling and writing career, I have witnessed that the most successful writers not only promote their current published books, but they also know that the best way to sell their existing books is to write and release new books.

But you can't write and release those new books if you don't write every day and make it a consistent habit, a common practice.

PROFESSIONALISM

ONE INTERESTING THING about writing is that there are so many different courses and workshops that teach a writer the craft of writing. But there's not nearly as many resources out there to assist a writer with the behavior that is associated with being a professional.

And, just for the sake of clarity, I'm not talking about a pro as being someone who receives money for the work they produce. I'm talking about the way a writer behaves and interacts within the writing and publishing communities and with fans; about reading and understanding different publishing-related contracts, meeting deadlines and commitments, operating within the conventions of an expected format or genre; about dealing with reviews, critics and adversity and maintaining an overall positive reputation.

The digital world created opportunities well beyond the restrictions that previously existed for writers. But it also, inadvertently, exposed a far wider realm of levels of professionalism, or perhaps lack of professionalism than ever before.

Perhaps, in the old school "gatekeeper" process of finding an agent and publisher and of getting work published, the large steps, restrictive processes and longer waiting periods allowed a writer the opportunity to acclimatize themselves to moving from hobbyist writer to professional. This isn't to say that the publishers offered their writers any training in this regard, nor that all people who have been or are traditionally published behave like professional writers; but perhaps the required actions such as the query letter, the manuscript submission process or even the pitching process had the side-effect of forcing some writers into beginning to develop those skills well before their work was actually published.

Of course, one side effect of this new world which allows virtually anybody the ability to create an account and click a few buttons and get their eBook onto the world's largest bookstore in a matter of hours, means that there are many "writers" out there who aren't actual writers, like you and me. They are simply using the same tools believing that they'll be able to make a quick buck. In the strictly traditional "gatekeeper" process of publishing, most of these people wouldn't have bothered, because of the intense work and waiting involved in that old process.

These "get rich quick" hucksters can give all of us writers a bad name; because their behavior is typically far removed from any desire to ever be a professional writer. But let's just ignore those people for now, except to say that, because you have taken the time to read an eBook like this, you already stand out as someone willing to invest not only in your writing, but in yourself as a professional.

Of course, just in case you are thinking that I am poo-pooing digital publishing in favor of the "glory days" of traditional publishing, let me share the flip side. Because there is another trend that has taken place in traditional publishing that didn't exist before. There was a time, long ago, where a writer could simply live like a hermit, pound out words on their typewriters, mail that manuscript to their editor or agent, and sit back, letting the system take care of the distribution and sales of their work. They never had to appear in public, nor did they even have to behave in a professional manner. The same gatekeepers that held back the flood gates of submitted manuscripts also protected some of their published writers from ever being revealed as awkward introverts who weren't skilled at interacting well with others. They also served nicely in terms of keeping the public unaware of which authors were just plain jerks.

Those days are gone. Even if you traditionally publish, your job isn't done once you hand your manuscript over. One of the criteria publishers pay attention to for the writers they contract is their presence, their engagement in social media, and their professionalism.

For the most part, regardless of whether you are traditionally published or are self-published, understanding and behaving professionally can be something that prevents you from being successful, or standing out as a consummate pro.

Below, I break professionalism down to three elements. "Paperwork, Contracts and Content," "In Person Appearances and People Skills," and "Adversity and Rejection."

Paperwork, Contracts and Content

Within traditional publishing there are templates, formats and behaviors associated with the query and submission process. There are boilerplate contracts. And there are publishers who only publish specific types of books or particular genres.

Taking the time to learn and understand all of these nuances demonstrates your professionalism and will save you a significant amount of time, and, most likely, frustration and heartache.

Getting a contract from a publisher can be an exciting thing; but understanding that the contract is a negotiation and thus something that is negotiable is an important element of protecting your long-term intellectual property (IP). Publishers will, of course, set out a contract that gives them everything they could ever possibly want, even if they don't plan on exploiting all those rights. It's okay to have a respectful discussion about some of the clauses that might be detrimental to you and your work.

A book that I strongly recommend writers read is *Dealbreakers* by Kristine Kathryn Rusch. I didn't discover the book until I had already signed my first contract with Dundurn for one of my non-fiction "ghost story" titles. Having worked in the industry for years, and understanding a bit about what I was doing, I had already made a few requests to their standard boilerplate contract that I was unwilling to sign. But, when it was time to sign the contract for the next book, having just finished reading Rusch's *Dealbreakers*, I found twelve more clauses that I asked them to change. The publisher responded by either removing or revising ten of the twelve clauses that I had an issue with. The two remaining ones I had asked to change were long shots, and weren't "make-or-break" for me, so I was quite satisfied with the result; and now they have a unique contract template for me for my books going forward. All thanks to the advice from Kristine Kathryn Rusch.

If you don't ask, you definitely don't receive.

And there is no harm in asking. Unless, of course, you ask in an unprofessional manner. When I wrote back to Dundurn, I was courteous and respectful. I didn't write a letter decrying they were bloodsucking scavengers and that I refused to sign until they removed that list of clauses. I outlined my hesitation at signing and, where applicable, explained my reasoning for each request.

And, even though the contracts with the various retailers, like *Kindle Direct Publishing* or *Kobo Writing Life*, or the digital distributors, such as *Smashwords* or *Draft2Digital*, are not negotiable, it is just as important that you read through and understand the terms you are agreeing to and perhaps even the rights you might be giving up.

For example, there is a common clause in all of the major eRetailer terms that you agree to when signing up. Sometimes referred to as the "most favored nation" clause, it states that you cannot sell the same eBook via another retail outlet for a lower price. If so, that retailer reserves the right to price match and take that lost revenue out of your share. Amazon is, perhaps, the only retailer that regularly and aggressively responds to violations of this term, but you should double-check the terms you signed up for at Kindle, Kobo, iBooks and the other retailers and distributors you are using, and you'll see that they all have some language to that effect.

Beyond contracts and agreements that you sign with others are the things that you do within your own "office" that are important, such as the research you conduct, for both writing and business purposes, as well as tracking expenses, submissions, publications, etc.

Successful writers are ones who do the necessary research for the creative part of their writing. Yes, there are particular articles and stories that don't require much research, because they rely on information the author already has or perhaps are derived completely from the imagination; but often times there are elements within a book that are best served by doing a little homework and being able to write about people, places and things with a little bit of understanding and perhaps even authority. That all comes from understanding the importance of effective research.

Research is also useful for writers who need to understand the layout of the worlds they are operating in. If a writer is pursuing a traditional publishing path, then researching the agent, editor or publishing house that they want to pitch their work to is critical. And, if they are pursuing the more DIY approach, research is required for learning how and what to do, which publishing professionals to hire, how the various retail and distribution channels work, as well as what strategies and promotion tactics work best for their particular niche, genre or product type.

Tracking not only your research, but your various writing and publishing activities helps you maintain an organized and professional perspective. For example, in traditional publishing, keeping a log or spreadsheet of what story or novel was submitted to which magazine, agent or publisher allows you to properly track where each of your stories or books currently are in their life cycle. Filing the signed contracts for and keeping account of when the rights you licenced to a publisher expire can help you when it comes time to leveraging those rights when another opportunity presents itself. Or perhaps understanding that you actually only sold North American rights to a publisher means that you still own the "Rest of World" rights and can use *Kindle Direct Publishing* or *Kobo Writing Life* to publish the work to other territories; this practice is becoming more and more common for many writers who, previously, were only exploiting their IP using traditional publishing.

Within self-publishing, tracking which titles are published to which retailers and through which processes, as well as the pricing that you have set in multiple currencies, to ensure that they are all priced consistently across the various global retail channels, is important. It might seem simple when you have one or just a handful of books, but, as your catalog grows and your use of multiple sources for the broadest global distributor increases, or even changes over time, it might be difficult to know how one particular book is being published to a specific online store.

Many of my own books, for example, are published via the following sources to get into as many outlets as possible in as many formats as possible:

- Kindle Direct Publishing (direct)
- Kobo Writing Life (direct)
- Google Play Books Partner Centre (direct)
- Draft2Digital (distribution)
- Smashwords (distribution & direct)
- PublishDrive (distribution)
- StreetLib (distribution)
- Direct Sales (via Bookfunnel)
- KDP Print (Amazon POD)
- Ingram Spark (POD distribution)
- Findaway Voices (production & distribution)
- ListenUp Audiobooks (production & distribution)

Keeping track of which platform is publishing to which retail channel is confusing. Now consider the multiple currency control that many of them offer. This is simple not something that can be trusted to memory.

Speaking of multiple currencies, attending to and paying attention to currencies well beyond the standard US dollar ensures that your eBook itself reflects a price that looks natural to a consumer in that territory.

It not only looks more professional but doing this strategically can help increase your bottom line earnings.

For traditional publishing, there is a specific expected format and process for how to send your work to be considered for publication. There are expected protocols within each step of the process. Understanding those is one key to success within that method of publishing.

When it comes to self-publishing, there are similar expectations that demonstrate professionalism. The expectation is that the work being published has been professionally edited, that it has been proofread, and that the marketing copy and cover design has been created with the target audience, or ideal reader in mind. These are processes that a traditional publisher is usually skilled at; although I regularly do have a say for those elements of my own traditionally published books – the difference is that I am not responsible for finding the skilled persons to create and work on them.

One final thought on the idea of contracts is being reliable and honoring your commitments.

Does your contract state, or did you commit to handing your manuscript over to your editor by a specific date? *Do so*. Did you hire an editor for your self-published work under a specific schedule of when they could expect to receive that work? *Hit that deadline*. Give these people a reason to want to work with you again, otherwise you'll be losing contracts or not being able to re-hire a great professional who helps make your work better, and you'll gain a reputation as being unreliable.

Did you put up a pre-order for a specific date for a self-published title? Then do everything in your power to upload the final version of that book on time. Sure, *Kindle Direct Publishing* will revoke your pre-order privileges for a year, but there are other consequences that affect your image. Think about the fans who have pre-ordered that book and what this missed deadline means to the people who invested in you and your book.

In Person Appearances & People Skills

I'm going to start with a few basics that you might snicker about because they seem to be givens. But it's not something to laugh about. It happens. More often than you might suspect.

Your personal appearance should adhere to some simple and common social standards and conventions.

Such as the basics of personal hygiene and grooming.

Yes, many writers are introverts and are perhaps most comfortable sitting in seclusion in pajamas or underwear they haven't changed for days. Or they relish in being eclectic and reclusive and unique in their appearance.

Eclectic and specific author branding is fine. I mean, as part of my horror and ghost-story writer brand, I make appearances with a life-sized skeleton named Barnaby Bones and typically wear dark clothes that feature skulls.

But there is being eclectic and making a decided effort to appear with a specifically curated brand, and there is basic hygiene that should have to go without being said. Sadly, I've seen it all too often that I feel it is worth stating.

Bathe or shower. Tidy your hair. Brush your teeth. Wear clean clothes.

This works well whether you are meeting with agents, editors, retail representatives, other writers, or readers.

And, while your outward appearance and the smell you project can have a detrimental impact upon your professionalism, so to can the manner by which you conduct yourself either in public or online.

Simply: Don't be a jerk.

Treat other people with respect and, whether it is through in person discussions, email communications or even comments left on various social media channels, conduct yourself with professionalism and grace. There are far too many stories of "authors behaving badly." You don't want to be considered one of them.

Think about someone that you met who was crass, rude, vulgar and unpleasant. Someone who had noting but negative things to say or hostile reactions to virtually any stimulus. Is that a person you enjoy interacting with? Is that someone you would want to invest time, energy or, as a reader perhaps, invest your hard-earned money in?

Don't be that person.

It's not just useful in your role as a writer, but it is also something of value for life in general. You never know when the person in front of you in line at the grocery store, for example, could be a reader, or potential reader. Or the random person sitting on the bus or plane beside you might be another writer, or work for a publisher or retailer you are interested in fostering a relationship with. People are more likely to share their negative impression of someone than to pass along praise. So, it is easy to make a bad impression and far more difficult to make a positive one.

As a bookseller and retail representative, I can tell you that I have gone out of my way to promote, push and share titles from authors whose behavior either towards me, or my witnessing of the way they treated others is professional, courteous and respectful. And on the flip-side I have purposely ignored, deleted messages from and even actively shared "warnings" to colleagues about those I have dealt with who are difficult, disrespectful and unprofessional. Which one of those would you rather be seen as by a bookseller?

No matter how people interact with you, or who they are, your behavior, actions and the things you say should reflect professionalism. You never know who is watching.

Or, more aptly, assume that everyone is watching all the time – and behave accordingly.

Adversity and Rejection

Rejection comes in many ways to writers.

In traditional publishing, it usually comes in the response to a submission. But in self-publishing, and even in traditional publishing, rejection can come in the form of negative reviews.

One thing to consider, and something I learned from fellow author Kerrie Flanagan, was that the work was not rejected. It, most likely, was merely something that was not right for that editor at that time, or, in the case of a negative review, that the reader wasn't the ideal target audience for that writing. Kerrie doesn't even like to use the work rejection. She feels it is too harsh and carries far too many negative connotations. But regardless, the truth is that you are not being personally rejected. Your writing is. That specific book, story or article is being rejected. And it is usually because there is a mismatch between the writer and the reader.

Common advice for authors is to never read the reviews of their books on sites like Goodreads or Amazon. It is good advice. And responding to reviews in any way, even in what you believe is a positive way, can easily be misinterpreted as you being a "defensive" author with thin skin.

But sometimes, if a writer learns how to accept or handle rejection or negative reviews, they can use that to further develop either their writing or their business practices.

I'll share two examples from my own experience. One from traditional publishing and another from self-publishing.

Early in my writing submission days, my desire was to have one of my horror stories appear in the respected and award-winning *Northern Frights* anthology series edited by Don Hutchison. Year after year I would submit stories to Don. And, year after year, he would reject the stories, often writing a line or two about what it was about the story that didn't work for him.

Don is a brilliant editor. He could, quite effectively, in just one or two sentences, point out something that a good developmental editor often helps a writer turn a good story into an excellent one. So, I often reflected upon Don's comments and applied them in a revision to the story. And, often, I ended up selling that story to another editor after following Don's advice.

Years later, and the first time I met Don at a book launch event in Toronto, he recognized my name and the first thing he said to me was: "Ah yes, Mark Leslie. I remember your stories. I'm sorry we never connected on any of them."

"Please don't be sorry," I replied. "In fact, I wanted to thank you. Because the comments you wrote back helped me revise and sell those stories to other markets. Your rejections have actually helped me improve my writing and helped my career as a writer."

I'm pretty sure that Don's impression of me improved upon that encounter. It's not often that an editor will ever hear a writer share something positive that came from having their work rejected.

Many years ago, I created a digital chapbook of a couple of previously published short stories about snowmen that were often well-received and adored by readers. I packaged them until the title *Snowman Shivers: Scary Snowmen Tales* and made it a perma-free title in order to attract new readers to my work. Over the years it received plenty of both positive and negative reviews. And, while I typically take negative reviews with a grain of salt, I did notice something in one of them. It said that the stories were well-written, but the stories were more dark humor than scary.

I realized that I had unintentionally misled readers or created the wrong impression. That reviewer was right. The tales were more *Twilight Zone* than horror, and, while they were indeed eerie, there was a strong undertone of dark humor to them. So, in mid 2018, I revised the eBook and updated the subtitle to something very specific and in line with the actual content. It is now called *Snowman Shivers: Two Dark Humor Tales About Snowmen*. My goal was to ensure that I didn't mislead or misrepresent the title and have the wrong reader picking it up expecting one thing but then getting another. And, ever since making that update, the downloads of this title have increased, and the accompanying reviews are from people whose expectations were more likely in line with the actual product.

Yes, reading negative reviews can be difficult, and responding to them in any way is something that is best avoided. But being able to step back and look at the review with a critical eye about how to make either the product, or the representation of that product, better, can be helpful. But only if you are able to step back and look at it, not as the creative writer with a heart of glass, but as the professional who is always striving to become better.

PATIENCE

I REALLY WANTED to put this element first on the list. Even though it's only the third, it felt like it took a long time to get here. This, after all, was the first element on my originally drafted up 3 P's of Self-Publishing success, so it's one that I not only had a bit of a soft spot for but was looking forward to sharing. This aspect, of all of the P's is one that can be applied within or toward each of the others; and it's something that a writer has to continue to continually struggle with throughout their career – *that* is just how important it is.

But I had to be patient.

No, I'm not just being cheeky by saying that. I want to ensure you understand the actual struggle to wait to dig into this element.

It was important that I first established two of the foundational aspects of practice and professionalism; because I think that patience is discussed in a more meaningful way once those two things were conveyed.

I'm sure you've heard the old adages of "Rome wasn't built in a day" or "Good things come to those who wait." Perhaps you are also familiar with the Stanford Marshmallow Experiment led by Walter Mischel in the late 1960s and early 1970s that found a correlation between children who were able to delay gratification typically displayed higher SAT scores, educational achievement and other life measures. That study, of course, was later re-conducted multiple times over the years to demonstrate a multitude of other factors that could sway the results, such as the child's trust in the experimenter or socio-economic factors, but it still revealed that there are those who are able to delay gratification and those whose tolerance for that was minimal. So, I'm not going to push on that particular experiment to support a correlation between patience and success. But I will argue that being able to wait for a long-term outcome perhaps makes it easier on a person.

Patience, of course, is a difficult thing to come to grips with, particularly when we live in a society where we possess access to a virtually endless stream of information, entertainment and resources via a device that is so portable we can hold it in the palm of our hand. When, with the push of a few buttons, we can have our eBook published to 190 countries around the world to thousands of retail channels.

I am, perhaps, lucky, in my experience growing up in what might be considered a much slower time. Because I didn't really have to choose patience. I had no choice.

Consider the immediacy of email versus the long-term experience of long-hand letter writing. Whenever I find myself impatient over an email that hasn't been returned after 24 or 48 hours, I often reflect back on the weeks and months between letters that were mailed back and forth between me and my friends. But email, of course, is still considered a much more archaic method of communicating when sending a text or a direct message usually goes right to a device that connects me directly to the single person I need to connect with, and *now*.

But patience, for a writer, in the early days, was a huge part of the overall experience.

Such as typing up a story and mailing it to a publisher and then waiting six months or more for a response. Then, if the story was rejected, having to return to perhaps re-typing it again to send to the next publisher. Or, if the story was accepted, waiting upwards of a year or two to see it published.

Back then, I simply had no choice. That's the way it was.

I learned to develop and hone my patience muscles.

And, even though I grew up honing those muscles, I still very easily fall prey to completely ineffective behavior such as logging on to my eBook sales dashboard and clicking refresh to see what eBooks I have sold since I checked it just a few hours ago.

Unless I have been running a successful promotion on one or more of my titles, clicking that refresh button is usually a disappointing experience. It might be akin to, back in those "olden" days, of sitting by the mailbox and waiting for the mailman to bring me that acceptance letter.

The reason I first lined up *Patience, Practice* and *Persistence* (the third of which we still have to get to) in that order in the first place, was because I regularly shared stories of how we usually only see or hear of a successful author once they have made it. And we rarely appreciate all of the practice and persistence and the patience they applied to attain that level of success.

Hugh Howey is a self-published author icon regularly held up as an example of how self-publishing could lead to fame and fortune. What isn't often shared is that, his breakaway novel, *Wool* was the tenth book he published.

Even within traditional publishing, it used to be that an author's career didn't really take off until after their third book was published. Authors, and their publishers, spent a much longer time waiting for that author's brand to slowly build; investing in a longer-term commitment to growing together with that author. And, in my discussions with various hugely successful self-published authors, they admitted that the didn't really start to see those "life-changing-opportunity-to-quit-the-day-job" style earnings until after their third book was published.

Now, of course, one of the main challenges in traditional publishing is that authors usually have to make or break it with their first book; otherwise, there is no contract for a second book.

When writers ask me the best way to sell their existing book, or books, I will typically tell them the best thing they can do to sell more copies of it is to write and publish their next book. This isn't to suggest the old Oscar Wilde adage that *nothing succeeds like excess*, but it is more to say that, instead of sitting and waiting around, being active and working on the next thing will help make that time pass more quickly; and, while you are at it, working at building your catalog of titles, the sales will build over time.

This isn't to say that you never have to engage in promotional activities, because that is a regular part of the process. Those often result in sales spikes and waves of higher volume. And it's not often that running a single promotion is going to have a lasting impact. But the combined effort of multiple promotions, spaced out over a longer time period, can have a lasting and positive impact.

But stepping back and planning out a long-term strategy for use of these types of promotions, rather than randomly throwing at targets on the fly requires a great deal of commitment and patience.

And, on the flip side, I would also argue that lack of patience most definitely contributes to limiting an author's success.

When I was working for Kobo, and my goal was to attract authors to publish their work to Kobo's catalog via Kobo Writing Life, I kept running into a situation that was as common as the persistent sound of coughs, sniffles and throat clearing in a quiet assemble of a large group of people. It was quite prevalent during a time early in the boom of self-publishing that's regularly referred to as "The Kindle Gold Rush."

An author, having already had success at Amazon, found out about Kobo, set up their titles on the platform, and then sat and watched their sales dashboard waiting for the magic to happen.

When nothing happened, even after repeatedly hitting the refresh button, they got frustrated.

Often, after less than a month, they would declare Kobo a dead or useless platform and then delist (unpublish) their books and go back to being exclusive to Amazon via Kindle Direct Publishing's *Select* option.

One of the things they failed to see was that on platforms like Kobo, iBooks and some of the other retailers, it took a little longer for the visibility and algorithms to kick in. It often took running a promotion, or even including links to retailers beyond Amazon, in order to start to gain some momentum with customers there.

For most authors, getting any traction on Kobo, could take months; typically, somewhere in the six-to-nine-month time period.

But impatience would usually get the better of them. And, as mentioned, the reaction to pull out and go back to Amazon exclusivity was strong in those ones.

Of course, when things weren't going as rockingly with their sales on Amazon after another 90-day tour of duty in KDP Select, they might re-list or republish their work to give it another go. Again, usually after a minimal time period, they would delist their titles and go through the cycle again.

One of the things they failed to understand was that every single time they removed their titles, the ranking, the algorithms, all the things in the back end within the retail systems that work at slowly building up the author and title rank would be reset back to zero.

So, every single time they pulled out, then came back, it was like starting over from square one.

(This is not even to mention, of course, the perspective this gives the retailer about that author's level of professionalism as a publisher)

The lack of patience, lack of willingness to give it a little time to slowly build their brand and presence on other retailers, led to a self-fulfilling prophecy that I believe will hurt them in the long run, if it hasn't already hurt them.

Because, before I left Kobo, one of the things I continued to hear from authors with whom I had, a year or two earlier, shared this type of advice with, would return and show me the sales charts that indicated the slow but positive direction their Kobo sales had taken, but only after staying the course for a longer period of time. For some authors it was just a few months, but for most, it was six or nine months before the sales curve started to trend in a decidedly positive direction.

Six to nine months can seem like an eternity when you are sitting and staring at the sales dashboard like a dog that spends the entire day staring at an empty food dish and waiting for their human to come home and fill that dish.

As Tom Petty sang, the waiting was the hardest part.

Wouldn't that time be much better spent invested in writing the next book?

Which is one of the reasons why the original 3 P's of *patience, practice* and *persistence* worked so nicely together. Not giving up, continuing to work at your craft and become a better writer and to produce new material not only gave you a larger catalog of titles to sell, but it made the time seem to pass in a different way, and thus expending energy on being patient was reduced.

PROGRESSION

THERE ARE TWO main types of Progression to explore here. The first is related to the craft of writing, and the second is about progression within the industry.

Progression in Your Craft

In the first of the P's we looked at the importance of practice, of continuing to write, every day, if possible, with the goal of using that to become better.

But, even though it's stated and, for some, assumed, the reason for practice isn't just the matter of fact "more words on the page" that result from it; it's the other thing that happens when a person continues to work at something.

It is progression. Improvement. Even if it is by imperceptible wins.

Though progression is the natural by-product of practice, it is important to split it out into its own unique element. That is how important it is.

Because just doing the same thing over and over, without improving upon and continually learning, is just doing the same thing over and over. If (to use a crude example) you don't understand the basics of grammar, you might continue to use the word "your" in the incorrect context when you mean to write "you're" (you are) in more sentences rather than learning and improving. ("Your never going to improve" VS "You're never going to improve.")

That is where working with an excellent editor can help. They can help you find patterns of habits in your writing that you don't notice, and which might be almost invisible to you, but which can be off-putting for a reader, perhaps even kicking them out of the narrative you are trying to lead them through. And yes, even the best writers still have well-formed habits and word pattern choices that can be jarring.

To consider this, (because it is often easier to see it in someone else than in yourself), think of a friend or an acquaintance you know who regularly peppers their every-day speech with a colorful word, or phrase. Maybe it's the f-word and its variations, typically just adding "ing" to the word, that they liberally sprinkle into their talk as an adjective and an adverb. So much that if you were to track and get a nickel for each time they use the word, after a short discussion with them, you'd have enough money to buy yourself a coffee or perhaps a more expensive alcohol-based drink; which could come in handy in terms of helping you deal with the excessive and repetitive f-bombs.

Or perhaps it's the insertion of the extraneous and un-necessary word "like" in speech. When I was growing up, excessive use of this word was an indicator of "Valley Girl" talk' but it has moved more and more into popular culture and modern speech from adults to children and even the well-educated, not necessarily for the creation of a simile, and not just as a mis-used adjective or adverb, but for dialogue attribution and as vocal "pauses" in speech itself. Taking a nickel from each use in some conversations could leave you with enough money to purchase an entire round of drinks. Which we could all, like, really use in, like, certain circumstances, right?

I used those two examples because they can be jarring and easily recognizable and are quite likely something you have experienced and can thus easily see (or "hear"). In your writing, the patterns and over-use of some words are likely to be subtler, but a good editor can usually help you detect them and hunt them down with an unforgiving and unrepentant red pen.

Yes, writing and writing and writing some more is a fundamental key. But there's a quiet and often unstated, or perhaps understated additional element to all that practice that comes with it. It is the ability to continue to learn and become better at your writing.

I think that the open-ness to learning, no matter how practiced, skilled, or proficient a person is, is an essential key.

I like to reflect on Neil Peart, the drummer from the Canadian rock band, RUSH. An inductee into the *Modern Drummer* hall of fame in 1983, making him the youngest person to ever receive that honor, Peart is often regarded as one of the best drummers to emerge from the rock world. Initially emulating the icons he grew up enjoying, drummers such as Keith Moon (*The Who*) or John Bonham (*Led Zeppelin*) and spending endless hours in his basement practicing playing like them, Peart developed his own unique style, inspiring an entire new generation of drummers. And yet, despite all the accolades, awards and honors, and having played drums for 30 years, in 1995 he stopped to re-learn how to play drums under the tutelage of Freddie Gruber, a legendary jazz drummer and teacher.

In a 2017 article in *Musicradar*, Peart is quoted as saying that Gruber helped him loosen up his playing. "That's what his coaching was all about," Peart said. "It was all physical, not musical. He's not the kind of teacher who teaches you to play the drums, he teaches you how to dance on the drums."

But that wasn't enough. In 2007, he continued to be a student, wanting to refine his skills and be able to do "big band" style drumming, in honor of the legendary Buddy Rich, so studied and re-learned drum timing techniques with Peter Erskine.

Regardless of how good he was, of how respected and successful he was, Peart never stopped learning, or re-learning the craft he loved so well.

So, taking a cue from Neil Peart, who re-learned how to dance on the drums, what are the ways that, through regular practice and continuing to learn and re-learn the skills of writing, are you willing to continue to master the fine art of making the words dance on the page?

A free weekly resource that I find extremely beneficial towards continuing to re-learn and focus on refining and honing my own writing craft is the podcast *Writing Excuses* which is hosted by authors Dan Wells, Brandon Sanderson, Mary Robinette Kowal and Howard Taylor.

The podcast, which mostly focuses on the craft of writing, is promoted as "fifteen minutes long, because you're in a hurry, and we're not that smart." It is meant to be digested in a format that can be enjoyed even on the shortest of commutes or while performing some other daily chore, such as doing the dishes or walking the dog. Even if the podcast ever stops producing new episodes, there are, as of this writing, thirteen seasons of incredible free backlist material that you can learn from.

Progression in the Business

If progression with the craft of writing itself is the foundation upon which you create a pathway to success, progression in understanding the business of writing and publishing allows you to build a structure that fits in with the current architectural trends.

The business of writing and publishing evolves. A little more than a decade ago eBooks weren't really a thing. Digital publishing involved print-on-demand (POD); there were no easy paths to self-publishing via Kindle, Kobo and the other eBook platforms. The Kindle and *Kindle Direct Publishing* didn't exist until 2007. *Smashwords*, the world's first major eBook distribution platform, wasn't founded until 2008.

If, today, you are considering your publishing and self-publishing options, and you haven't learned all that has changed and been made available to writers since 2007, then you would still be only looking at the old way of doing things. Your paths would, for the most part, be to either work at finding an agent and/or publisher to sell your book to, or paying a ridiculous amount of money to a vanity publishing outfit to have the book self-published using POD technology.

I know that is a bit of an exaggerated example, but I wanted to use it to illustrate a point.

Just as you, as a writer, are constantly changing, growing, and evolving, so too is the business of writing and the business of publishing.

I have been working in the bookselling, writing and publishing professions since 1992, and I have witnessed some dramatic shifts. But, as much as I already have experience and information and insights, I am still, every single day, reading and listening to and watching developments in our industry; and I am focusing not just on self-publishing, but also on traditional publishing – because both are constantly changing and evolving.

Around the time that the Kindle and digital publishing was emerging, New York Times Bestselling author Kevin J. Anderson, a writer of about fifty books with millions of copies in print started to detect a shift in the industry, and gathered together with his wife, fellow author Rebecca Moesta, and friends David Farland, Eric Flint, and Brandon Sanderson to discuss the changes and to help teach one another the new elements from the publishing landscape so they could better navigate those changes.

Those meetings eventually became *Superstars Writing Seminars*, where Anderson, the aforementioned colleagues and James A. Owen come together every year at a gathering in Colorado Springs, CO, not just to teach the business of writing and publishing to between one hundred and two hundred writers in a very intimate and interactive setting, but to also continue to learn about the industry themselves.

Anderson and his colleagues aren't just teaching, but they are continuing to learn. If you can look at a group of writers who have millions of copies of their books in print, are published in multiple languages and been on the New York Times bestseller lists too many times to count, and yet recognize the importance of continuing to learn, then there are, indeed, things you and I can continue to also progress within our own learning.

PERSISTENCE

LET'S START BY pausing to look at a proverb that you are likely familiar with. It has been traced back to a teacher's manual written by American educator Thomas H. Palmer in 1840 and a song popularized by William Edward Hickson in 1836.

It's a lesson you should heed,
Try, try again.
If at first you don't succeed,
Try, try again.
Then your courage should appear,
For if you will persevere,
You will conquer, never fear,
Try, try again.
Once or twice, though you should fail,
Try, try again.
If you would at last prevail,
Try, try again.
If we strive, 'tis no disgrace,
Though we do not win the race;
What should you do in that case?
Try, try again.
If you find your task is hard,
Try, try again.
Time will bring you your reward,
Try, try again.
All that other folk can do,
Why, with patience, should not you?
Only keep this rule in view,
Try, try again.

It is, indeed, a lesson you should heed. I included the full lyrics not just because I find them inspiring, but because the pattern of the full set illustrates another important element. While most people are familiar with or recall the most well-known first few lines from this phrase written almost two hundred years ago, there is a lot more to it than just those bits that remain in popular use.

The same is true for the behind-the-scenes work, and the persistence involved in success.

People only see the end result, the tip of the iceberg, as it were, and not all the behind-the-scenes work.

I spent a good portion of the past twenty years working in the I.T. sector of the book industry, (managing the database for Canada's largest book retailer, importing data feeds from publishers as well as working at Rakuten Kobo, Canada's answer to Kindle). Those environments exposed me to strong elements of high tech and start-up culture as well as Agile development, where the mantra for success is to fail fast and fail often.

But it's not a new concept.

I think about all the mini-failures that go towards putting on a play for public performance. The actor, standing there, missing their cue, a blank look on their face before shouting out, "Line!"

Many mistakes, many failures, many errors happen along the way. It's part of the process of putting on a show.

When I was in university, I was actively involved with the theater company there. For the hundreds of plays that I worked on during my time there, I saw many of them from the audition and first reading phase, through the scene practices, the costume fitting, the set building, the lighting blocking, the sound cues, the seemingly endless train of rehearsal after rehearsal, until, finally, after months of work, the full dress rehearsal and then opening night.

The audience, of course, only saw the final show, after it was all put together and after most of the errors and messy bits had been tidied up.

One main difference between theater and writing and publishing is that most of that "prior to opening night" work happens within the realm of the mind and the page, and instead of a large crew of actors and backstage folks, there's usually the writer, one or more editors, perhaps some mentors, advisors, coaches or other professionals, sometimes a publisher and their crew, some first-readers, and maybe an entire cast of voices in various stages of the writer's mind filling them with self-doubt.

Again, the end result is the published work.

And, occasionally, the end result is the huge success that only the outside world sees.

The outside world never sees the work that went into it.

Nor do they see the multiple failures, false starts, and re-tries that happened along the way.

Because I cut my teeth in writing back before self-publishing was even a viable option, I was trained in the art of persistence as I typed up and packaged my stories and mailed them off to publishers. I remember readying statistics that it took an average of thirteen submissions of a story to different magazines before receiving an acceptance. And, in the tracking that I did for my stories over the years, I found that estimation was pretty accurate. Yes, sometimes I would sell a story on my first submission. But often, it took a half dozen submissions before I made a sale. And, occasionally, twenty or more times of sending the story, getting a rejection, then doing it all over again. The average, I found, was in the twelve to thirteen range.

I took a quick look back at my old tracking documents, and I can see that for at least a dozen of those stories that were eventually published, if I had given up after just one or two rejections, they might never have actually been published. There were only perhaps half a dozen tales that were accepted at the first place I had submitted to.

If I had given up after my first rejection, I might only have published about six short stories, and would never have had enough previously published tales to collect into my 2004 book *One Hand Screaming*, which was my first foray into self-publishing.

Within the realm of self-publishing, while there aren't curators and gatekeepers preventing a work from being published, there are roadblocks that come in the way of a work being published but not selling in any sort of "successful" manner. The lack of sales, or lack of positive reviews are among the things that a writer looks at similar to rejection, and some allow that to discourage them to continue, rather than to persist in their writing and publishing.

In the chapter on patience I brought up Hugh Howey and the fact that his breakaway best-selling title, the one optioned by Ridley Scott and where he sold the print-only rights to a major publisher, *Wool*, was his tenth published book. Not only that, but Howey started writing his first novel when he was twelve years old, and didn't complete his first draft until he was thirty-three.

Before he stepped away from the writer conference scene, I spent quite a bit of time with Hugh. Both of us traveled in the same writer conference circuits. Also, on one of his trips to Canada, I was his unofficial chauffeur to several Toronto-area visits and speaking engagements, including an intimate evening for writers at the Kobo HQ.

A couple of the analogies that Hugh regularly shared, and which resonated quite effectively with me involved basketball and local bands.

Imagine, Hugh would say, your favorite big-name basketball player attempting to learn to play basketball with a million people watching. Or imagine if the very first pickup game they ever played in was his only chance to land an agent and get signed to the NBA. And yet, this is the type of pressure that writers put on themselves all the time. They forget of the thousands of practice games these NBA all-stars put in, of the dozens of years playing almost every single day of their lives working hard at getting better. These are the things that we don't see. These are the behind the scenes endless hours of work, and persistence, that led to where they are.

He also talked about local indie bands who would practice in their garage every weekend during high school, then perform, perhaps for free, in local community centres for teen dances, then work for either free drinks or a modest flat fee to perform in various local bars; all the while busting their butts, practicing and working hard without seeing any sort of profit or big break. They persist, they keep at it, and, occasionally, once they sign a big deal or one of their songs hits big, people never see the years of hard work and of not-giving up in the face of adversity. They only hear the #1 single.

I really like those analogies, because they are a reminder of how the success we see comes after a long string of hard work and never giving up.

What if Hugh had given up after his first, or even his second book?

What if J.K. Rowling had given up when, after more than a dozen rejections from publishers, she hadn't persisted and continued to write her passion project about a young wizard living with muggles who wasn't aware of his true destiny?

"It is impossible to live without failing at something, unless you live so cautiously that you might as well not have lived at all," Rowling says. "In which case, you fail by default."

Bella Andre, who had been a hard-working mid-list writer producing books with a traditional publisher, received a huge slap in the face when her editor informed her the next three books she had planned centered around the "Sullivan" family she was so keen on writing, were not accepted.

With no contract, she could have given up.

But she didn't. She worked hard. She persisted. She brought in an 8-figure income from her writing, and, similar to Howey, signed a record-breaking print-only deal that allowed her to keep her digital book rights.

From failure and rejection to success through hard work.

"If you just keep at it," Andre says, "work long hours, and pay close attention, magic will happen when you least expect it."

PARTNERSHIP

WRITING IS, OF course, a solo activity, or at least a mostly solo activity. A writer sits in front of a blank page or a blank screen with either a pen or pencil in hand or their fingers gently resting atop of a keyboard and they set about composing their words. No matter if they are writing in a quiet personal space or sitting in the middle of a bustling coffee shop, the main activity is taking place between the writer's mind and that blank document in front of them that they are filling up. Even in co-authored works, which are the most obvious form of partnership, each writer still usually performs their task in solitude.

But collaborations among authors have become more and more common, and perhaps this is something that writers might think is more applicable in today's world than it used to be. But when you reflect upon it, you'll perhaps see that partnership was always an important element of a writer's success.

Let's start by looking at how successful writers use partnerships in today's digital environment and then work our way back.

In the past several years, one of the ways that authors have been using partnerships is in their marketing efforts to grow their reader base, to increase their unit sales, to rank high on the retail webstores and to reach the prestigious lists such as the *New York Times* or *USA Today* bestseller lists.

Partnerships, or collaborations in this area involve the bundling of multiple eBooks into multi-author box sets that are usually within a particular theme or genre. These can be done with the authors working together to create a single ePub file that contains all the books from the authors involved, with an agreed-upon method of distribution, price and royalty-splitting structure and with each author marketing that digital box set to their audiences via their newsletters, social media and other out-reach. But they can also be done through third party companies that curate these types of bundles such as *StoryBundle* or *Humble Bundle* or perhaps using a more DIY and self-driven tool such as *BundleRabbit*.

Collaboration and partnership don't have to be as structured nor involve longer-term commitments. Virtual communities are places where an author can dip in and out, where they can ask questions or offer advice, suggestions or share their own experiences. They have become a popular way that authors collaborate today.

One of the first most prominent virtual communities that authors have been able to turn to are the *KBoards*. Initially branded as Kindle Boards, a community for Kindle Users and Authors, the name and intent later evolved to discussion of digital reading regardless of device or platform, and a more extensive discussion in the "Writers' Café" section, where authors regularly read and post information.

There are hundreds of other public groups, many of them appearing on social media sites like Facebook. Some of them are generic and some of them focus in on a specific theme or approach to publishing.

The *20Booksto50K* group, for example, was born out of a concept Michael Anderle derived from his initial self-published eBook income; he calculated, based on an average annual income of $2,500 for his existing eBooks, that if he could publish 20 books, he would be able to earn $50,000 in a year. He didn't just prove that model: he exceeded it, earning well into the six-figure mark before he reached 20 books.

The *Author Support Network* is a more generic group that isn't tied to a specific methodology of publishing and was created by Marie Force as a place for indie, traditional and hybrid authors to share information and ideas in a supportive, nurturing environment. Similar to the *20Books* group, it is meant to be a supportive community where authors can learn, share and grow as well as support one another.

The International Indie Author was created by and is overseen by Mark Williams, who is regularly acknowledged as one of the foremost authorities on global publishing as it relates to indie authors. It is a unique group in that, unlike so many others, it isn't centered on Amazon and sales in the US and the UK. Instead, the focus is on markets well outside the "Western" markets and the information shared here and via *The New Publishing Standard* e-magazine/website (a collaboration between Mark Williams and Antonio Tombolini) reminds authors that publishing does not happen in isolation and takes a very global and holistic approach to information and perspective sharing.

Other, longer term and more formalized partnerships would include the creation of branded groups, such as *The Jewels of Historical Romance*. These twelve internationally best-selling authors have been banded together for years to combine their marketing efforts to their very similar target audiences to offer great monthly prizes and a Facebook Salon where their readers can mix and mingle and talk about their favorite subject, and where they can combine their marketing dollars into the creation of branded materials for both their fan base as well as the retailers that they work with.

When I was at Kobo, the *Jewels* sent me and a few other folks at Kobo a beautiful glass treasure box with an engraved plaque on it filled with candy and a note to hang onto it because there would be more candy coming. Every quarter or so, they would send a printed newsletter update that featured information about forthcoming titles from their dozen members, usually along with a treat package: a wonderfully brilliant bag of Hershey's kisses that were branded as "kisses from the Jewels." The newsletter content was similar to the info packages that really good sales reps from publishing or distribution companies would send to retailers as reminders about some of the titles that bookstores should be ordering in, or, in the case of a digital retailer like Kobo, of the titles they might want to consider in their new and forthcoming release merchandising campaigns.

Partnerships don't need to be formalized by collaborative publishing activities or branded groups. One of the most amazing things about the rise of self-publishing and indie-publishing communities in the past half-dozen years is just how willing most authors are to engage with other authors, ask questions of one another and to openly share things that are working, or not-working for them. This underlying sense of community can be a real life-preserver to an author who can, in today's world of choices and the fire-hose of information, feel like they are getting into water that is well over their head.

Of course, while the digital world has made it easier to connect with other writers, there are still similar groups through local libraries, bookstores and community centers. In the mid 1980s, for example, long before the internet, and back when I was hammering out stories on an old *Underwood* typewriter, I remember struggling to find other writers to connect with in a remote mid-Northern community of under 2,000 people. But, even in that small population, I was able to find a writing group that met on a semi-regular basis.

But, even back then, and well prior to that, writers found success via other types of collaborations.

These are the types of partnerships related to both the craft and business of writing. They involve working with an editor or a teacher to learn and hone the craft of writing. They involve working with an agent to help sell the work into the publishing market. They involve working collaboratively with a publisher's editorial and promotions staff. They involve interacting and engaging professionally with libraries, bookstores and representatives from the various digital publishing platforms.

All of these require elements of partnerships, of people working together collaboratively towards common goals that usually are about making your work better and then getting it into the hands of as many target readers as possible.

Of course, the final element of partnership blends so naturally in with the next P on our list; it is the fundamental partnership that happens between the writer and the reader.

PATRONAGE

THIS ELEMENT is perhaps one that writers might think is more applicable in today's world than it might have been decades ago. They would be right in thinking that, but I'm not just talking about crowd-sourcing from places like *Patreon*, *Kickstarter* or other crowd-funding services; that is definitely a part of this. I'm talking about the overall idea of patronage. Of willing consumers.

It was Kevin Kelly who first introduced the concept of *1,000 True Fans* in a 2008 essay.

In case you aren't familiar with this concept, Kelly stated that, to be a successful creator able to make a living off of that craft, you don't need millions of dollars, or millions of customers, clients or fans. You just need one thousand *true* fans who will buy anything that you produce, sight unseen. These are the fans who would drive hundreds of miles just to see you, who would willing lay down big dollars for the "unabridged" or "exclusive content" version of something you produce; they will buy the print book, the eBook and the audiobook version of your book. They are the die-hard or super-fans.

Kelly's concept brilliantly gets into the math, which many people overlook, because they might have heard the concept but don't understand the details. And I talk about that more later on in this section.

But I'm getting a bit ahead of myself. Let's go back to the simple definition of the term *patronage*.

Patronage, according to the *Canadian Oxford Dictionary*, is "the support, promotion, or encouragement given by patrons." And, while we're exploring terminology, that same source defines patron as "a person who gives financial or other support to a person, cause, arts organization, work of art, etc."

That's a great start for us to look at those three elements of patronage, starting with that last one first.

Encouragement

A writer needs readers. It is a beautifully natural symbiotic relationship that might even draw comparisons to the old thought experiment: *If a tree falls in the forest and there is nobody there to hear it, does it make a sound?* In this case, though, it might go something like this: *If a writer writes a story and there is nobody there to read it, how does the writer make a living as a writer?*

That's right, apart from the philosophical bent on this thought experiment, there's a transactional one.

Therefore, when writing, a writer needs to keep in mind the target audience for their work. Who is this story, this non-fiction, ideally for? It is critical that a writer consider this target audience, even if, during the writing of the work itself, the writer's desire is to write a book that they themselves would enjoy reading. The entire goal, in keeping the target audience in mind is to fully and properly understand their expectations and seeking to meet those expectations. Who are they and why would they read this story or book? What are they hoping to get out of it? Will this writing provide them with what they are looking for? Meeting these expectations is the best way for a writer to get to a place where that right audience responds in an encouraging way.

Encouragement, of course, comes in multiple forms. The first, and most obvious one, is the actual purchase or download of the content in question. Ideally, it is followed by the reading or consumption of that content.

Of course, encouragement, at a much higher level, would include things such as leaving a positive review for that work on an online bookstore or on *Goodreads*, signing up for the writer's author newsletter, or even reaching out to the writer to ask when their next book is going to be available.

All of those elements, usually combined and mixed in different ways, provide the underlying external encouragement that helps to fuel a writer's progress.

Promotion

Beyond merely reading and indicating that they are interested in reading *more* of a writer's work, of continuing to be a consumer of their work, through things like leaving positive reviews, or signing up for the author's newsletter, is the actual act of promoting a writer and their work.

It's one thing to leave a positive review of a book. It's another to actively want to share their enthusiasm for it.

Have you ever finished reading a book and loved it so much that you couldn't help but want to tell every single person you encountered how much enjoyment or value you got from it? How, having read it, you felt permanently altered? Have you ever finished a book and then had to stop yourself from forcefully putting it into the hands of every single one of your friends? Have you bought extra copies of the book just to gift to other readers you know would love it?

That's the type of reader response I'm talking about; one that leads, naturally, to the organic desire, in that reader, to want to promote you and your book or books.

For years in my early days of bookselling, I would constantly keep stock of Richard Laymon's *One Rainy Night* in my store. And, when I encountered a horror fan who was okay with extreme and graphic adult content, horror, gore and violence, I would put the book into their hands and tell them that if the book wasn't one that begged to be read in a single sitting, they should bring it back and I would gladly personally buy the copy off of them. That is because, at home, I always had an extra copy of the book on hand; with the right reader, I would loan a copy of the book, knowing full well that I was likely to never get that book back. I never did get any of the books I loaned back; nor did I ever have a customer return to do anything other than want to buy more books by Richard Laymon.

And, while that might be a bit extreme, that is the type of reader promotion that leads to that step-up level of patronage.

Within this element are such things as a writer's street team; the folks who are so enthusiastic about your writing that they want to spread the love and share your work with others. They are like independent sales reps for you, your book and perhaps your author brand.

These are the people that you want to give extra attention, support, and care to. They are likely also the people you should be willing to give your work to for free. Before you panic and say: "But they are a true fan; they're willing to buy it. Why would I want to give them that work for free?" Consider the fact that, if they are that true of a fan, they'll end up helping to sell multiple copies of whatever book you gave them for free. Some of the core, true and die-hard fans will also end up purchasing the book they got for free, either just to show their love and support, or perhaps in order to gift a copy of it to someone they think will love it.

Support

Apart from being willing to purchase, review and be enthusiastic about your writing, are the fans who are willing to invest in you long term. Support, of course, begins with the reader being willing to provide cash for the product.

But it can go further than a simple transaction per unit basis.

Sometimes readers want to invest in an author in a way that helps ensure they continue to produce the content that they value.

This is where crowd-sourcing and funding opportunities such as *Kickstarter*, *Go-Fund-Me*, or *Patreon* might come into play.

Earlier I mentioned, Kevin Kelly's concept of *1,000 True Fans*; and I promised I would get into the math. Because this is where the rubber hits the road.

Kelly's concept starts with 1,000 fans each willing to spend $100 a year and for which you make 100% margin. That is to get to $100,000 earning per year. If your target income is $50,000, then that means 500 fans spending that much. Or, if the margin you earn on a product is $50, then the fan base number changes to 2,000. If the margin, or profit is $5, then that becomes 20,000 fans. I'm sure you can see, now, that to apply this for a writer changes some of the numbers. It's not always 1,000 fans.

To use a personal example, I earn about $2.00 for every print book that my publisher Dundurn sells. At 1,000 True Fans who buy one of my books every year (I usually publish one book a year with Dundurn), I would earn $2,000. Of course, if the book was co-authored (several of my Dundurn books are written with another writer), that becomes $1,000. But I also self-publish. And if those fans all bought my $4.99 eBook, I'd earn about $3.50 off that. That would be $3,493. Add $2,000 and you have almost $5,500.

So, in the case of a writer like me doing a single traditionally published book and a single self-published book a year, I would need about 18,000 fans, each willing to purchase about $30.00 worth of my books per year at retail, which results in my approximate $5.50 per fan margin or profit.

So, yes, 1,000 true and die-hard fans are critical, but so, too, is the rate of production and the value for each item. There are multiple ways to play with these numbers.

One of them is to produce a lot more content.

Another is to sell direct. If I sold those same items with a retail value of $30.00 in a way that I kept 100% of the margin (yes, I'm doing simple math here and not bringing in the delivery mechanism or payment processing costs), I could do it with about 3,333 fans instead of 18,000.

More and more creators are taking advantage of either selling direct or using a fan-funded approach to help them earn additional revenue.

Apart from the additional margin in the creator's pocket via these sources, there's also an underlying fundamental emotional and personal investment that the reader, or fan, feels. They have invested in this creator. Therefore, they want to see this creator succeed. Because they are intelligent and perceptive and make excellent decisions. They wouldn't, after all, invest in a writer who wasn't worth that investment.

A while back, there is a musician whose songs I adore, who created a *Kickstarter* campaign to raise the $75,000 she needed in order to hire a producer that she wanted to work with but couldn't afford. Her name is Alicia Witt and her campaign name was called *15,000 Days* (representative of her age when the album would be produced). Having been a fan of this independent musician's work for several years, I jumped at the chance to show financial support to make that new record happen. Not only did she reach her goal, and I rec'd my lovely "die-hard fan" bonus swag and content, but I got to follow the progress she was making along the way while producing her EP and truly felt a part of it all. Heck, I have shared, multiple times on social media my excitement for the recent release of the EP, but, despite having free digital downloads and a copy of the CD, I've also purchased each single release in order to further show my support (and do my little bit in helping each new release rank higher so that other potential fans might discover her music). I not only invested money into this product, but I invested time and energy into talking about and promoting Alicia and her wonderful music. (As an aside, my connection with her has involved other unexpected and unplanned perks such as Alicia giving me permission to have her appear in a minor walk-on role in my forthcoming book *Fear and Longing in Los Angeles* as herself, and including excerpts from lyrics as the book's hero, Michael Andrews, goes to a bar where she is playing music and ends up having a quick casual chat with her that helps him come to terms with a relationship challenge he is trying to deal with.

Other creators are using *Patreon* as a way for avid consumers of their content to be able to subscribe to them. Some writers are writing fiction, for example, not to be sold to an agent or publisher or not to be self-published and sold through Kindle or Kobo or other eRetailers. Instead, it is meant to be read only by their patrons, their die-hard and core fans.

Of course, regardless of how a patron supports a writer: direct purchases, support via a crowd-funding application, or purchasing their products and perhaps also being enthusiastic about promoting and supporting that author's work, you'll see why patronage is one of the key elements of publishing success.

PROMOTION
(The Not-So-Silent Silent P)

SOMETHING THAT YOU might have considered was sadly overlooked in the many P's that have been discussed, but one that has snuck its way into the content multiple times throughout the 7 P's, is a basic and underlying activity that most successful authors engage in.

Promotion.

I kept struggling with wanting to pull it out into its own element, but I also couldn't help but see it as a fundamental part of every single other elements that I discussed. That being said, now that I've outlined all of the 7 P's I'm calling out *promotion* to remind you that it's there, and that it's a part of each of those previous elements.

- *Practice:* Learning how to run different types of promotions and then trying them again and again, exercising those muscles
- *Professionalism*: Ongoing interactions with booksellers, retailers, industry professionals and other writers in a manner that promotes you and your author brand in a positive manner with a solid impression
- *Patience:* Realizing that it often takes more than a single promotional activity to have a positive effect and also the planning, scheduling and waiting involved
- *Progression:* As you practice and try new promotions, you need to analyze, revise and adjust in order to fine tune what works and chip away the things that aren't working
- *Persistence:* You need to try and fail and retry different promotions, never giving up on the idea of promotion even if you give up on specific types of promotions that aren't working for you
- *Partnership:* Working with other authors collaboratively, engaging the services of third-party promotion sites, finding mutually beneficial ways to promote your books and a particular retailer

- *Patronage:* Offering your best, most loyal customers unique freebees or content that nobody else has access to, or even ensuring they hear about promotions well before anybody else

I'm not going to go into detail about specific promotional activities, because there are entire books about marketing and promotions that a writer can engage in.

But, regardless of whether your book is self-published or traditionally published, promotion is a critical aspect for sales. Yes, there are more opportunities for price discount style promotions (ie, using services such as *BookBub* or *BargainBooksy*) when you own all the rights and completely control the price of your book; but that doesn't mean there aren't many things you can do to promote your traditionally published books. I regularly engage in different promotional activities for each of the types of books that I publish. Since my traditional books tend to sell better in print than in eBook, most of my promotional activity in that regard is focused on the print book. And, conversely, since my self-published titles bring in far more revenue from digital sales, my promotional efforts for those are geared towards that.

Promotion, of course, begins even before you publish, or perhaps even finish writing, your first work.

I harken back to my friend James A. Owen, who shares, in a very popular talk he gives every year at *Superstars Writing Seminars*, a wonderful lesson in an experience he had with eggs benedict in a hotel restaurant. Without giving away the brilliance of his story (because it is best heard through the man's eloquent rendition of it), the message James ultimately expresses is that nobody every inspired anybody else to greatness by pretending to be less awesome than they really were. A writer should own and be proud of the things that they create. Thus, promotion always begins by believing in and being willing to promote yourself, and not deliberately holding yourself back.

CONCLUSION

THIS WAS AN interesting book to write. It started off as a concept that I planned on using for a single chapter in my book *Indie Publishing Insider Secrets*. But, as I was writing the first draft of that book, the chapter kept growing and growing. When I hit 10,000 words, even before turning the book over to my editor, I realized that I was going to have to cut that chapter down to a simpler, more summarized overview of the 7 P's of publishing success.

So, I did that.

But in the process of cutting and refining the content down, I kept seeing elements from the unabridged version that I felt were useful. When I showed that original first draft version of the chapter to my editor, they asked why I didn't consider revising that chapter into a mini stand-alone eBook, with each of the P's becoming their own chapter. That is the brilliance of working with a professional editor or having a second or third pair of eyes to bounce your writing off of: perspective.

Speaking of perspective, that was another P that was left on the "cutting room floor." Perspective is important, both internally as well as working with others so that you can learn from their perspective. It's an important element within the craft of writing, since a writer often has to consider perspective in every scene they create. But, my editor called me out on my desire to keep adding P's as the resistance against ever finishing this project, so we decided that perspective might be another one of those mostly silent P's that would chug along and empower the big seven. More than once, my editor suggested cutting the P's down to five to make remembering them easier, in the same manner that the original 3 P's so easily rolled off the tongue.

"Perhaps it would make the package more *portable*," they said, not only playing upon the P theme but inserting a little stab at my fondest for alliteration.

I laughed and then started to rhyme off from a list of half a dozen other P's that, like *perspective* I had already cut from the original draft. "Purpose, Prestige, Practicality-"

"Okay," my editor said, cutting me off. "I get it. Seven is the magic number."

Can you take a guess at what those other P's might be?

The main reason I am sharing this discussion about the format, the number and the behind-the-creation of this short book, is to illustrate the fact that the 7 P's are an artificial construction. That construction is designed to make some underlying principles a bit more memorable and digestible.

It is something that many articles, books and self-help gurus have used for years. Consider: *The 7 Habits of Highly Successful People* (Covey), *The Five People You Meet in Heaven* (Albom), *The Fifth Discipline* (Senge), *The Seven Spiritual Laws of Success* (Chopra), *The 4-Hour Work Week* (Ferris), *The 48 Laws of Power* (Greene).

Yes, I truly do believe in the principles for publishing success that you have just read. I have either personally experienced, or witnessed other writers using them to carve out success in their writing careers. But I took those elements I believed in and purposely re-constructed and molded them into the 7 P's (okay, maybe even the "buy 7 and get 1 free" P's if you prefer) that are outlined in this text.

My hope is that, on your own writing and publishing path, you take the time to consider your relation and your position with respect to each of those elements, and how you might be able to re-adapt and prescribe them into your own plans for a most successful author journey.

RESOURCES

BELOW YOU WILL find a short list of either some of the resources that I called out and mentioned, or ones that I have found helpful in my own writing and publishing journey. I could, for example, list 100 books that I found extremely useful, or the dozens of podcasts I regularly listen to, but I didn't want to create an exhaustive list – merely, a place where you could get started.

Books

Million Dollar Professionalism for the Writer – Kevin J. Anderson & Rebecca Moesta, WordFire Press, 2014.

Dealbreakers: *Contract Terms Writers Should Avoid*, Kristine Kathryn Rusch, WMG Publishing, 2013.

The Author's Guide to eBook Bundling: *Level up Your Income With the Power of Bundling*, Chuck Heintzelman, Kydala Publishing, 2016.

On Writing: *A Memoir of the Craft*, Stephen King, Scribner, 2000.

Podcasts

Writing Excuses
www.writingexcuses.com

The Creative Penn
www.thecreativepenn.com

Stark Reflections on Writing & Publishing
www.starkreflections.ca

Websites

The Alliance of Independent Authors –
www.allianceindependentauthors.org

Writer Beware
www.writerbeware.com

Facebook Groups

Author Support Network

www.facebook.com/groups/AuthorSupportNetwork/

20 Books to 50 K
www.facebook.com/groups/781495321956934/

The International Indie Author
www.facebook.com/groups/441469159372773/

ABOUT THE AUTHOR

Mark's highly successful experience in the publishing and bookselling industry spans more than three decades where he has worked in almost every type of brick and mortar, online and digital bookstore.

The former Director of self-publishing and author relations for Rakuten Kobo, and the founding leader of *Kobo Writing Life*, Kobo's free direct-to-Kobo publishing tool, Mark thrives on innovation, particularly as it relates to digital publishing.

He writes full time and mentors and coaches authors and publishers about digital publishing opportunities both 1:1 and via his Stark Reflections on Writing & Publishing weekly podcast.

You can learn more about Mark at www.markleslie.ca

Selected Books by the Author

Under the name Mark Leslie Lefebvre
Writing & Publishing
The 7 P's of Publishing Success
Killing It on Kobo
Indie Publishing Insider Secrets

Under the name Mark Leslie
Non-Fiction ("Ghost Stories")
Macabre Montreal
Haunted Hospitals
Creepy Capital
Tomes of Terror
Spooky Sudbury
Haunted Hamilton

Fiction
Nocturnal Screams (Short Fiction Series)
A Canadian Werewolf in New York
Evasion
I, Death
Active Reader: And Other Cautionary Tales from the Book World
Bumps in the Night

As Editor
Fiction River: Superstitious
Fiction River: Feel the Love
Fiction River: Feel the Fear
Fiction River: Editor's Choice
Tesseracts Sixteen: Parnassus Unbound
Campus Chills

Did you love *The 7 P's of Publishing Success*? Then you should read *Killing It On Kobo: Leverage Insights to Optimize Publishing and Marketing Strategies, Grow Your Global Sales and Increase Revenue on Kobo* by Mark Leslie Lefebvre!

Do you want to increase your overall sales and visibility on Kobo?
Are you having trouble gaining any traction or growing your reader base outside the Kindle store?
Wouldn't it be empowering not to be dependent upon a single retailer for the majority of your eBook income?

If you want to tap into the mind behind the creation of Kobo's world-class self-publishing platform, Kobo Writing Life, to understand both the basics and some of the complexities of the platform, then look no further.

Mark Leslie Lefebvre was the Director of Self-Publishing and Author Relations at Kobo for six years. Kobo Writing Life was born out of his own desire as an author to establish an author-centric free publishing platform. Drawing upon insights from his years at Kobo as well as his previous two decades of bookselling, writing and publishing experience,

Lefebvre shares the challenges, quirks and tricks that are important for helping you leverage Kobo's strengths to your advantage. In this book you will learn:

- How to navigate the Kobo Writing Life dashboard as well as Kobo itself
- Strategies to optimize your metadata to increase both sales and visibility
- The importance of leveraging Kobo preorders by understanding how they work
- Ways to maximize your margin and global earnings per unit sale
- Proven price optimization techniques that the most successful authors use
- How to increase your chance of promotional sales direct at Kobo. . . and more . . .

Killing It On Kobo is an in-depth, heart-felt and eye-opening series of insights collected in a single volume to give you full access to information and proven strategies that you can use to maximize your own sales and ultimate success selling through Kobo.

www.ingramcontent.com/pod-product-compliance
Lightning Source LLC
Chambersburg PA
CBHW031310060426
42444CB00033B/1166